The
Railway Age

The Railway Age

L. W. Cowie

First published in 1978 by
Macdonald Educational Ltd
Holywell House
Worship Street
London EC2A 2EN

© Macdonald Educational 1978

ISBN 0-382-06296-5
Published in the
United States by
Silver Burdett
Company, Morristown, N.J.
1979 Printing
Library of Congress
Catalog Card No. 79-64162

The author and publishers would also like to thank David Jenkinson, of the National Railway Museum in York, for his help in preparing this book.

Contents

The first railways

▼ The London–Brighton mail coach is caught in a snow storm on Christmas Day 1836. Before the days of rail travel, journeying by stagecoach could be extremely uncomfortable.

At the beginning of the 19th century most people did not travel far from their homes: it was much too difficult and expensive. There were few good roads, and most people walked from place to place. For long distances there were stagecoaches, but these were not very convenient. The horses were changed every 16 kilometres and a coach could travel over 160 kilometres in a day, but it only carried 12 passengers at a time, and the journey was cramped and uncomfortable as well as costly.

Even on the best roads, horses could not carry very heavy loads. The only way of transporting goods was by boat – along rivers and canals. The boat was pulled by a horse which walked along the bank, and travelled about three kilometres an hour. In the 18th century, in north-east England, horses were also used to pull coal trucks along rails from coal mines to cargo boats at river quays. This could be called an early form of 'railway'.

George Stephenson worked as a fireman at a colliery which was served by one of these early 'railways'. He was in charge of the steam engine which pumped water out of the mine. The steam engine had been invented in the 18th century, and, in 1814 Stephenson built a steam locomotive which was as powerful as forty horses. It hauled coal along a railway track to the River Tyne.

◀ Iron railway lines were built in northern England in the 18th century. Horses hauled coal trucks along them from the mines to cargo boats at the quayside.

▲ Ralph Allen built this railway at Prior Park early in the 18th century. It was used to transport building stone to Bath from Allen's quarries at Combe Down.

◀ An excited crowd gathers to watch George Stephenson's steam engine, *Locomotion*, haul one of the first trains at the opening of the Stockton and Darlington Railway in September 1825. The directors of the railway company travelled in the carriages.

▲ A miner walks home from work. Behind him is the locomotive which was built in 1812 by John Blenkinsop for the Middleton Colliery near Leeds in Yorkshire. The locomotive hauled itself along by means of a cog operating along a toothed rack on the rail track.

In 1821 George Stephenson was hired as an engineer by the Stockton and Darlington Railway Company, who were planning a railway to run from the coal mines at Darlington to the wharves at Stockton-on-Tees, a distance of 64 kilometres. He persuaded the railway company to use his steam locomotive on the line instead of horses. He believed that 'Engines made after a similar plan will yet entirely supersede all horse-power upon rail roads'. When the railway was opened in 1825, Stephenson's engine did not burst as many had feared it would, though its chimney became red hot before the end of the journey. It pulled a train of more than 30 wagons, some loaded with coal and others fitted with seats for passengers.

England was at this time fast becoming an industrial country: the first in the world. Coal mines, shipyards, cotton mills and other factories were being built, and towns were growing much larger. The expanding towns and new industries needed a cheap, fast and convenient way to bring coal, iron and other raw materials to the factories, and to send the finished product to the ports; to take people to work and to bring food to the towns. The new Stockton and Darlington Railway was just one example of a means of transport which, as part of the Industrial Revolution, was to transform society, at first in Britain then all over the world.

The start of an era

A year after the opening of the Stockton and Darlington Railway, a group of businessmen decided to build a railway to link up Manchester and Liverpool. The line would carry all sorts of goods, and regular passenger trains were also planned to run between the great northern town and its port.

George Stephenson was appointed to build the railway. The promoters, however, were critical of his plan to take the line across a huge peat bog known as Chat Moss. A surveyor told Stephenson: 'There is nothing, it appears, except long sedgy grass and a little soil to prevent the railway sinking into the shade of eternal night.' At first Stephenson found that everything – ballast, casks and timber – did indeed disappear into the bog, but he persevered and at last succeeded in making a floating platform out of hurdles interwoven with heath upon which he could build an embankment.

Stephenson also found it difficult to persuade the promoters to use steam engines on the line. A Liverpool merchant said to him: 'It has been proved to be impossible to make a locomotive engine to go 10 miles an hour, but if it is ever done I will eat a stewed engine-wheel!'

However the promoters eventually agreed to offer a prize of £500 for the locomotive which they thought best suited for their railway. A competition was held at Rainhill, near Liverpool, in 1829. Four engines were entered for it. All at first did quite well, but by the second day only the *Rocket*, built by Stephenson's son, Robert, had fulfilled all the conditions of the competition. The promoters awarded it the prize and decided to buy all their engines from the locomotive works which the Stephensons, father and son, had established at Newcastle-upon-Tyne.

▲ The *Novelty*, a locomotive which competed at the Rainhill trials, proved too light to hold the rails.

▲ The *Sanspareil* used too much coke, making it too expensive to run.

▼ Stephenson's *Rocket* won the competition at Rainhill because it was the only locomotive to fulfil all the railway company's requirements.

▼ A train on the Liverpool and Manchester Railway crosses over the Duke of Bridgewater's Canal near Salford. There were 63 bridges under or over the railway on the 48 kilometres of track, more than on any other railway line of this length.

By the time the Liverpool and Manchester Railway was finished, eight locomotives had been built at the Stephenson works, and, in 1830, they all took part in the opening ceremony, pulling carriages which together contained more than 600 people. The trains set out from Liverpool and passed through the deep ravine of Olive Mount, up the Sutton incline and over the great 9-arched Sankey Viaduct. Here, crowds of onlookers had gathered, who gazed up with admiration and wonder as the engines passed noisily over their heads, puffing out thick smoke and showers of sparks. The passengers waved excitedly to the crowds from the carriage windows as the train clattered across the viaduct.

The trains reached a speed of 38 km an hour (24 mph), and at Parkside, 27 kilometres from Liverpool, the engines stopped to take in water. Here the horrified spectators saw the first fatal railway accident. William Huskisson, a Member of Parliament, got down from a train on to the line to speak to the Duke of Wellington who was in another carriage. He stumbled over a rail and was knocked down by the approaching *Rocket*. George Stephenson himself attached a coach to another engine, the *Northumbrian*, and drove the dying man back to Liverpool, in the incredible time of 25 minutes. In the midst of the tragedy, the amazing speed of this journey made people realize that a new era in transport had begun.

▲ Admiring passengers wait to board the trains at Edgehill Station near Liverpool.

▲ A locomotive takes in water at Parkside. The first fatal railway accident happened here.

The railway boom in Britain

During the 20 years which followed the opening of the Liverpool and Manchester Railway, literally thousands of miles of railway were built in Britain. As new railway companies were formed and new routes planned, towns and villages tried hard to ensure that the line would pass near them. People began to realize that they needed the railway in order to be prosperous; that without the railway their towns would become isolated and decline.

Building the railways was not always easy. Many landowners did not want the lines to run through their estates and ordered their gamekeepers to keep the surveyors out of their property. 'I was threatened with a ducking in the pond,' said one surveyor. 'We had a great deal of the survey to take by stealth when the people were at dinner. We could not get it done at night, and guns were discharged over the grounds to prevent us.'

Money for railway construction came from people who bought shares in the new companies. Investors could make a good income from a successful company, though of course they could lose all their money if the company failed. Railway companies needed a great deal of money to finance construction work. There were many problems: the builders might come across tougher rock or find that bridges needed deeper foundations than had been expected, and this caused delay as yet more money had to be raised.

IRELAND

▼ On 3 May 1830 crowds of onlookers gather to cheer the opening of the Canterbury and Whitstable Railway. By the middle of the 19th century most main towns in Britain were linked by rail.

▶ In 1837 Kilsby Tunnel (top) was built five miles south of Rugby for the London and Birmingham Railway. (Left) A painting of the Great Western Railway's important goods shed at Bristol.

▲ The engine shed at Swindon built locomotives for the Great Western Railway.

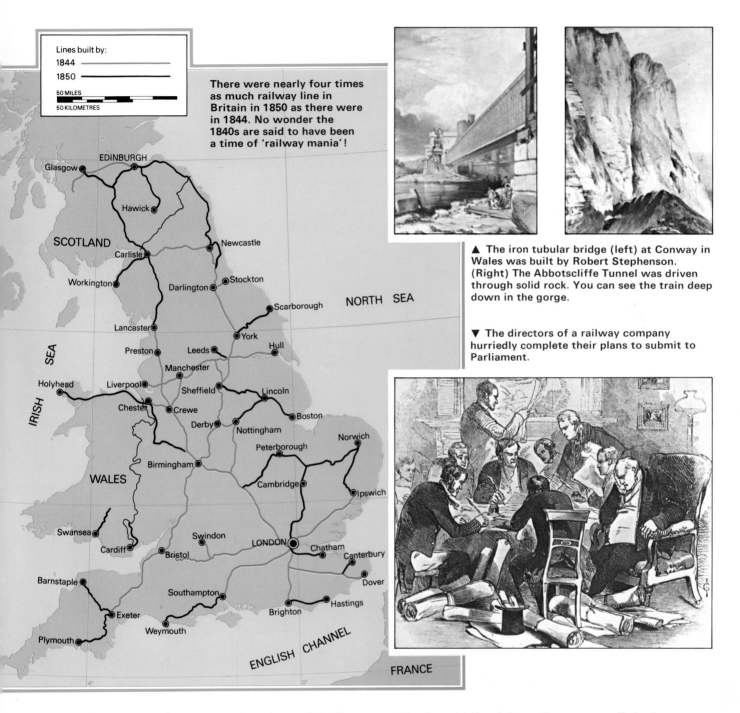

Lines built by:
1844 ——————
1850 ——————
50 MILES
50 KILOMETRES

There were nearly four times as much railway line in Britain in 1850 as there were in 1844. No wonder the 1840s are said to have been a time of 'railway mania'!

EDINBURGH
Glasgow
Hawick
SCOTLAND
Carlisle
Newcastle
Workington
Darlington
Stockton
Scarborough
NORTH SEA
Lancaster
York
Preston
Leeds
Hull
Manchester
Holyhead
Liverpool
Sheffield
Lincoln
Chester
Crewe
Boston
IRISH SEA
Derby
Nottingham
Birmingham
Peterborough
Norwich
WALES
Cambridge
Ipswich
Swansea
Swindon
LONDON
Chatham
Cardiff
Bristol
Canterbury
Barnstaple
Dover
Southampton
Hastings
Exeter
Brighton
Weymouth
Plymouth
ENGLISH CHANNEL
FRANCE

▲ The iron tubular bridge (left) at Conway in Wales was built by Robert Stephenson. (Right) The Abbotscliffe Tunnel was driven through solid rock. You can see the train deep down in the gorge.

▼ The directors of a railway company hurriedly complete their plans to submit to Parliament.

The 1840s were known as the time of 'railway mania'. The opening of a new railway was always a great event. The official train, whistling loudly, steamed into the terminus which would be brightly decorated and packed with cheering crowds. From the station the passengers walked in procession under a triumphal arch to the town hall where a celebration banquet was held. For the railway workers and their families a cold meal was served in a marquee erected on a nearby playing field. This was usually followed by sports and country dancing and finally by a firework display. It was the sort of day that people remembered for a long time after.

By the middle of the 19th century, all the important towns in Britain were linked by rail to London and to each other. For the first time in history there was fast cheap travel for everyone. The journey from London to Glasgow had taken a week by stagecoach. A few years later, by rail, it took only 13 hours.

All over the country, stagecoaches made their last run. Coaching inns were closed. Roads became deserted and fell into disrepair, as did the canals. For both passengers and goods, the railway in Britain became the unrivalled means of transport. From Britain the railway age spread to Europe and to America.

Early railways in Europe

The experiments with steam locomotives in Britain in the early 19th century aroused a great deal of interest in Europe. However there were not any existing colliery lines, as there were in Britain, on which steam locomotives could run. The first European steam locomotive was built in the Prussian Royal Iron Foundry in Berlin in 1815 but it was purely experimental and never left the works yard.

The first proper railway in Europe was a 60-kilometre line connecting Lyons and St Etienne in France. It had two steam engines, which were built by Marc Seguin, a French engineer who had visited England and studied George Stephenson's engines. Seguin tried to improve on Stephenson's designs by adding fans, which were driven by the wheels of his engines, to make the fire burn more strongly. However he soon found that this did not work; a train needs extra power when it is climbing uphill, and Seguin's fans only made the fire burn more fiercely when the train was running downhill and did not need extra power. For the lines between Paris and St Germain, opened in 1837, and between Paris and Versailles, opened in 1840, the French ordered locomotives from the Stephenson works at Newcastle; and the earliest French railways were built under the supervision of British engineers.

▶ Two trains which ran between Lyons and St Etienne on the first railway in France. The railway was opened in 1829. A passenger train (top) descends the slope between St Etienne and Givers, and (below) a train of coal-wagons is drawn by a locomotive.

▼ A French cartoon of 1832 caricatures a group of angry stagecoach drivers. They watch a crowded railway passenger train steaming past their inn and realize that soon there will be no more work for them. Their noses grow long with envy.

▼ The Archbishop of Paris blesses a locomotive in Le Havre station. Many people were afraid of the railway and the Rouen/Le Havre line was opened only after a religious service had taken place on the platform.

In the early days of European railways people were afraid of the new invention. When the Rouen and Le Havre railway was opened in 1847, for example, the railway company arranged for the engine of the first train to be blessed by the Archbishop of Paris before it left Le Havre station.

The first railway in Germany, the short Ludwigsbahn between Furth and Nuremberg, which was opened in 1835, obtained a locomotive – *Der Adler* – from the Stephenson works. It arrived for the opening day complete with a top-hatted English driver, William Wilson. He aroused great interest during the opening ceremony. He spent the rest of his life driving trains in Bavaria and was considered so important that he was paid a higher salary than the company's managing director.

The first railway in Holland, between Amsterdam and Haarlem, was built in 1839. Many Dutch landowners were opposed to the railway. In 1847 a squire near Delft refused to have a level crossing over his carriage drive, so the railway company built a detour. Soon afterwards the squire agreed to accept the level crossing, perhaps because of the noise of trains shunting by day and night on the detour around his estate.

European governments took an active part in railway construction and most European railway builders had an easier time than engineers in Britain. There were fewer road bridges; and bridges and tunnels were larger than in Britain. European locomotives and carriages could also be larger because European engineers allowed more ground clearance. This made cornering easier and helped to stabilize the train when travelling at speed.

▲ The opening of the first railway in Germany, between Furth and Nuremburg, in 1835. William Wilson, an Englishman, drives the locomotive, *Der Adler,* as it draws a train of 1st, 2nd and 3rd class passengers.

▼ A cartoon illustrating the way a Dutch railway company treated a landowner who refused to have a level-crossing built over his carriage drive. His house is almost surrounded by the noisy loop-line!

15

Early railways in America

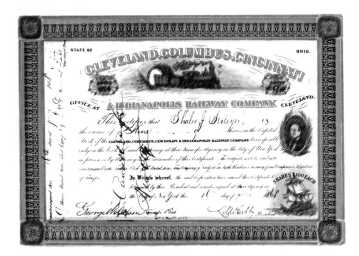

◀ An $100 share certificate in an American railway company. It was issued in 1868.

▲ Workers building the Northern Pacific Railroad across the Great Plains. Railroad workers in America had to face many hazards. Indians did not like the 'iron horse' being driven across their land, and often attacked the line. The US army was called in to guard the workers.

In 1829 a railway was built from Carbondale to Honesdale in Pennsylvania. A steam locomotive, the *Stourbridge Lion*, was imported from England; but the engine was too heavy for the iron-covered wooden rails and it only ran once.

The next year *The Best Friend of Charleston,* the first successful American steam locomotive, drew a train between Charleston and nearby towns. After 6 months it blew up when a fireman sat on the safety-valve to silence the hiss of steam. It was the first fatal railway accident in America.

In 1830 there were 50 kilometres of track in America. Twenty years later there were 15,000 kilometres. The railway had proved to be the quickest way of opening up the interior of the continent to new settlers and new industries.

American engines had to be powerful, for they had to climb steep gradients. Guiding wheels and under-carriages on a pivot (known as 'bogies') were added to European-type locomotives and carriages so that they could negotiate the sharp curves that existed on many American lines.

Carriages were longer than in Europe, and compartments were abandoned in favour of open saloons. In the mid-1830s the English actress, Fanny Kemble, found that American carriages had end doors and 'a species of aisle in the middle for the uneasy to fidget up and down, for the tobacco chewers to spit in and for a whole tribe of itinerant fruit and cake sellers to rush through!' In 1842 the novelist Charles Dickens called an American train 'a great deal of wall, not much window, a locomotive engine, a shriek and a bell.'

As the railway reached out across the vast continent, it faced many hazards: blizzards in the winter, prairie fires in the summer; buffalo herds sometimes delayed trains for hours on end; Indians attacked them as they crossed their land, and robbers held them up at gunpoint as they had done with stagecoaches in the past.

Yet these dangers did not prevent the construction of a transcontinental line to span the country from the Atlantic to the Pacific oceans. The Union Pacific Railroad was built westward from the Mississippi basin. The Central Pacific was built into the mountains eastward from California. Rival construction gangs laid tracks across desert wastes, wooded plateaux and precipitous mountains.

The two advancing railways met in Utah in the winter of 1869, but they passed one another and continued to lay parallel tracks, each hoping later to be able to claim as much of the line as possible. Eventually the government decided that Promontory Point should be the official meeting place, and there the last spike was driven in. The railway which would ensure the unity of the American States was completed.

► Chinese labourers built this timber trestle bridge in 1877 to carry the Central Pacific Railroad across the western slopes of the Rocky Mountains.

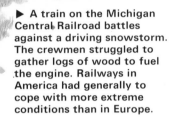

► A train on the Michigan Central Railroad battles against a driving snowstorm. The crewmen struggled to gather logs of wood to fuel the engine. Railways in America had generally to cope with more extreme conditions than in Europe.

▼ In 1869, the locomotives of the Union Pacific and the Central Pacific met at Promontory Point in Utah. After the golden spike has been driven into the last rail, the chief engineers of the two lines shake hands to celebrate the creation of America's first transcontinental railroad.

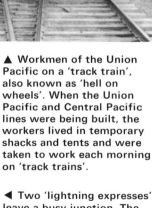

▲ Workmen of the Union Pacific on a 'track train', also known as 'hell on wheels'. When the Union Pacific and Central Pacific lines were being built, the workers lived in temporary shacks and tents and were taken to work each morning on 'track trains'.

◄ Two 'lightning expresses' leave a busy junction. The engines of these trains burned wood fuel. They made long journeys with few stops. This illustration is by the famous American printmakers, Currier and Ives.

Building the railways: the engineers

Richard Trevithick

1771–1833

▶ **Trevithick's railway at Euston in London.**

Richard Trevithick was a Cornish mining engineer. He was the first great pioneer in the development of the railway, and the inventor of the steam locomotive. In 1796 he built a steam carriage which he tested secretly at night along the lonely country lanes of Cornwall. The sound of hissing steam terrified the local people, who believed it was the devil passing by their cottages.

In 1804 Trevithick built the first ever steam railway locomotive. In 1808 he demonstrated another engine, called the *Catch-Me-Who-Can*, on a circular track at Euston in London. It pulled a little open carriage at about 12 kilometres an hour. People paid money for rides on it. After a few weeks it was derailed, and too badly damaged to be repaired.

George Stephenson

1781–1848

George Stephenson built the Stockton and Darlington Railway and the Liverpool and Manchester Railway. With his son Robert, he also designed the *Rocket* engine. One reason for Stephenson's success was the care he took in his work. When he built the London and Birmingham Railway, he is said to have walked the distance between the two towns 20 times.

The locomotive works which he and his son founded at Newcastle produced many steam locomotives, and the two men built a number of lines. Robert was especially skilful at designing bridges. One of the finest of these was the Britannia tubular bridge over the Menai Straits in North Wales.

◀ **George Stephenson carefully instructing his navvies.**

Matthias W. Baldwin

1795–1866

▲ One of Baldwin's locomotives.

Matthias Baldwin was an American engineer, and one of the most famous designers of railway engines. He built many similar locomotives which all used the same parts, and this practice was soon followed throughout the world. When he died in 1866 his works in Philadelphia were turning out 120 engines a year. They soon became the largest engine manufacturers in the world. By 1955, when the last Baldwin steam engine was built, they had made 75,000 locomotives. Some are still running today.

Isambard Kingdom Brunel

1806–1859

Isambard Kingdom Brunel was chief engineer to the Great Western Railway whose lines stretched from London westwards. Between 1835 and 1841 he built the line from London to Bristol.

Brunel was always ready to try out new ideas. He persuaded the Great Western Railway Company to use the newly-invented electric telegraph. This caused a sensation in 1845 when an escaping murderer boarded a train at Slough, only to be arrested, to his great surprise, at Paddington Station, where the police had received news by telegraph of his escape.

◀ Brunel's Box Tunnel near Bath.

Louis Favre

1826–1879

One of the great engineering achievements of the 19th century was the construction of the St Gothard railway line through the Alps, to link Lucerne in Switzerland with Milan in Italy.

Louis Favre began the construction in 1872. He had to build the line 1200 metres above sea level, through mountains where in winter huge avalanches crashed down into the valleys. On parts of the line he built galleries to protect the track, but the greatest protection was given by the St Gothard Tunnel. The tunnel was 15 kilometres long. It was driven through the heart of the mountain range and was, when completed, the longest tunnel in the world. The workers tunnelled from each end and the survey of the route was so accurate that when they met in the middle they were only a few centimetres off course. Favre died of a heart attack in the tunnel shortly before the opening ceremony.

◀ Building the St Gothard Tunnel through the Alps.

Building the railways: the navvies

▲ Building a railway line

1. A survey is made of the route for a new railway line.

2. Navvies level the ground with spade and pick, and load the earth into trucks.

3. Wooden sleepers are laid on a bed of flint or of stone chippings.

4. Iron rails are fixed on to the sleepers and bolted together.

5. A train steams slowly along the track to test it.

◄ Navvies building the retaining wall of a cutting at Camden Town in London. It is from a series of railway lithographs by J. C. Bourne, some of which are also reproduced on pages 12-13. As can be seen from this illustration, Bourne was fascinated by the enormous scale of railway construction.

Gangs of men called 'navigators' had built the canals in Britain during the 18th century. Local people crowded to see these men, who became popularly known as 'navvies'.

Many of the workers who built the early railways had previously worked as navvies, so this name was soon used to describe all the men who worked to build the railways. Navvies came from all over the British Isles, many of them from Ireland. As soon as one line was finished, they tramped on to the next job which might be more than 100 kilometres away. They became a familiar sight in the countryside – strong, burly men with clay-tinted clothes, tightly-laced high boots, and a piece of string tied round each leg below the knee. On Sundays and holidays the navvies liked to change their rough everyday working clothes and wear brightly coloured waistcoats, large neckcloths and knee breeches.

During the 1840s there were many thousands of navvies working on lines in different parts of Britain. They lived in wretched conditions in huts erected along the lines they were constructing. When the railway was being built on the south coast, in Devon, the hulks of old wooden warships were towed up river for them to live in.

People respected the navvies, but they also feared them. They were a rough, tough lot, who were loyal to each other and cared little for anyone else. A farmer wrote about them: 'More than 100 of them in this village were paid on Saturday and a pretty row there was. They were all drunk together, and some fought in the meadow for nearly an hour. The same night the villains stole all my poor neighbour's chickens, and there is not a fowl or an egg to be got hereabouts.' Country people often dreaded the arrival of the navvies, and were glad when they moved on.

◀ A jokey look at a navvy of 1865, 'ready for anything'! The pick, shovel and wheelbarrow are for work, the cutlass for fighting, the lantern for poaching and the jar for beer.

▼ Blasting rocks during the excavation of a cutting, another lithograph by Bourne. Navvies were often injured or killed by these explosions that could easily go wrong.

Navvies were better paid than most workmen. They certainly earned their money. The railway builders expected them to do their work quickly and would not employ them unless they did. In those days there were no excavating machines to help them. Everything had to be done by hand. They worked in gangs alongside a number of horse-drawn trucks, two men to each truck. With pick and shovel one would undercut the side of the cutting, bringing down the earth and rock, which his companion would load into the truck. Two men were expected to fill 14 trucks a day with 30 tons of rubble. No wonder they ate and drank in such quantities!

When the Paris to Rouen railway was built in 1841, 5,000 British navvies were sent from Southampton to prepare the line along the valley of the River Seine. In France the navvies amazed and alarmed the people as much as they had done in England.

The great age of steam

At the beginning of the 19th century it took as long for a person to travel from Rome to London as it would have taken a Roman living 1,500 years earlier.

Almost everyone was affected by the invention of the steam locomotive. It transformed society and marked the beginning of a new age.

In 1850 *The Times* newspaper wrote: 'There are thousands of our readers, we are sure, who, in the last three years of their lives, have travelled more and seen more than in all their previous life taken together. Thirty years ago not one countryman in one hundred had seen the metropolis. There is scarcely now one in the same number who had not spent the day there. Londoners go in swarms to Paris for half the sum, and in one third of the time, which in the last reign would have cost them to go to Liverpool.'

At first the idea of these terrible 'iron monsters', hurtling through the countryside at unprecedented speeds, had alarmed people, but soon the sight and sound of them became welcome and even magical. A farmer spoke of the first time he saw a train go by him in the fields: 'The white steam shooting through the landscape in the trees, meadows and villages, and the long train, loaded with merchandise, men, women and children, rolling along under the steam. I had seen no sight like that; I have seen nothing to excel it since. In beauty and grandeur, the world has nothing beyond it.'

It was a great excitement to see a train cutting its way through the night, as the red sparks flew from its chimney, the fire glowed in the engine and the bright lights flashed through the carriage windows. Many people, old and young, wanted to get close to the engines themselves and examine these strange and wonderful machines. Previously the ambition of many boys had been to be a coachman and handle a team of four fine horses on the road. But after the coming of the railways, most wanted instead to be an engine-driver, to stand at the controls in the locomotive cab as it went hurtling through the countryside.

◀ An early morning ride on the *Oliver Cromwell*, a standard Brittania class locomotive.

▶ A Dixiana narrow gauge locomotive running through the giant redwoods in the Santa Cruz mountains near San Francisco.

▼ Train spotters travel to inaccessible regions of Portugal to see this German engine built in 1910 and still running.

◀ Steam trains are kept in running order at the Bellows Falls Museum in Vermont, USA.

▼ The *Mayflower* steams through the English countryside.

Towns and the railway

The years when the railways were being built were also a time when towns were growing. The railways and the growth of large towns in the 19th century were both part of the Industrial Revolution, which had begun with the invention of the steam engine in the early 18th century. The Industrial Revolution led to the development of towns as centres of industry, to the mass production of goods in factories and to the construction of a railway network.

The railways could transport goods and people cheaply and quickly, bringing in raw materials and taking out manufactured goods from the factories, transporting people to and from and between towns.

By 1860 the focal point in many towns was the railway station. This was where travellers arrived and left the town. Near the station was the railway hotel, often magnificent and usually built by the railway company.

Along the lines from the railway station were signs of the changes the railway had brought. There were goods yards to which long trains of trucks carried food, coal and supplies of all kinds for the town. There were factories, workshops, breweries, warehouses, gasworks – all built near the track so that they could easily use the railway to transport their coal, iron ore, grain, cotton, or manufactured goods.

There were rows of new houses, probably no longer built with local stone, but with cheaper bricks and slates which had been brought from another part of the country by the railway.

There were other indications of the influence of the railway on town life. Before the railways each town kept its own local time. Afterwards, in order to plan their timetables, railway companies standardized the time to be the same throughout the country. Soon everyone was using this 'railway time'. People no longer had to rely on stagecoach travellers to hear the latest news; the railways brought up-to-date newspapers to every town. Mail was also carried far more quickly than before.

As a result of the railways the quality of the food available in towns was improved. Previously herds of cattle had been driven long distances to towns where they were slaughtered for meat; the meat was usually tough because the animals were thin from their journey. The railways brought fresh meat and vegetables, and fresh fish, not previously known in inland towns. Although a few cows had been kept in cellars, milk before had always been scarce; the railways ran special early milk trains every morning bringing fresh milk from the country.

The large towns of the 19th century would not have grown up without the railways. For the first time people could easily obtain goods not produced locally. The railways made possible a way of life that town-dwellers today take for granted.

▲ Railway companies built large hotels next to the railway station.

▼ Workshops multiplied as the railway brought in new customers.

▼ Overcrowding created slums as many people moved into towns to find work.

▲ The coming of railways transformed towns all over the world.
  The top of this illustration shows a town before the Industrial Revolution. The church is at the centre of it. The picture underneath shows how industry and the railways changed the town. The town grew larger. Factories were built, and also gasworks, warehouses and rows of new houses for the factory workers. The railway station with its goods yards was the point of arrival and departure for everything and everyone. It became the focus of activity in a growing industrial town.

RAILWAY TIME

Before the railways each town had its local time. To plan timetables, railway companies had to make sure that time was the same everywhere. Soon everyone used 'railway time'.

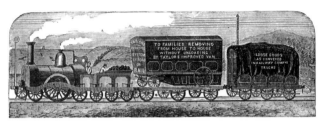

▲ Before the railway, horses were used for haulage. These two engravings show the effect the coming of the railway had on one furniture removal company.

▼ As a result of the Industrial Revolution and the coming of the railways, towns grew rapidly. Often their growth was influenced by the actual line of the railway.

▼ Many acres of land in the town became goods yards.

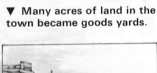

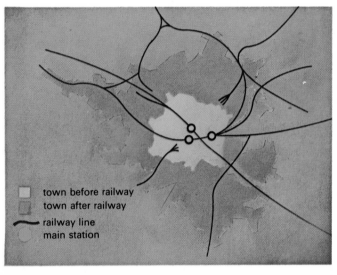

town before railway
town after railway
railway line
main station

◀ The railways transported goods quickly and cheaply. They changed the way of life in towns. For the first time people could easily obtain goods not produced locally. Fresh food was brought in from the country, fresh fish from the sea. The latest news could be read in up-to-date newspapers.

Railway architecture

From the beginning of the railways, engineers had to cope with all sorts of new building techniques.

The first stations—such as the Liverpool Road Station, Manchester – just consisted of one or more platforms. Ticket offices, waiting rooms and store rooms were added later, together with roofs which covered at least part of the platforms. Even in the earliest days, many large stations were built with lofty arched roofs, which gave shelter and allowed smoke to escape from waiting locomotives.

Combining iron with glass to span the roofs of these main line stations was an important innovation. The weight of the roof was supported by a lattice of great iron arches which were embedded firmly in the ground. The spaces between the arches were filled in with sheets of glass fixed to metal glazing bars so that the roof was thin, yet very strong, keeping the weather out but letting in plenty of light.

Often the roof was divided into 3 arches, as at King's Cross Station in London, or the remarkably modern station in Milan, Italy. Sometimes, particularly in countries with low rainfall, a station roof served to collect water for the locomotives. One way of collecting water was to support the roof with hollow cast-iron columns through which rain water drained into underground storage tanks.

These station roofs were practical and, with their wide sweep of iron arches, very pleasing to look at; but people in the 19th century did not appreciate what railway engineers were doing. They often preferred stations to be designed in familiar architectural styles. For instance, in front of the great roof of St Pancras Station in London is the massive Victorian Gothic St Pancras Hotel, which has gables, turrets and a tall, slim clocktower, and looks as if it were part of a medieval palace.

▼ **How a railway arch is built**
Ready-made, standard-sized latticed iron arches are erected on the site of the railway station or engine shed.

The upper spaces between the arches are filled in with sheets of glass fixed to metal glazing bars. As glass is not heavy, the arches can support a very wide span.

Near the ground the spaces are filled in with brick walls, which can be thin and have large windows because they are not needed to help support the weight of the roof.

▲ The 9-arched Sankey Viaduct. Until the coming of the railways scarcely any viaducts had been built since Roman times.

▼ A dramatic photograph of a train crossing the Forth Bridge. Notice the enormous steel girders and stone piers.

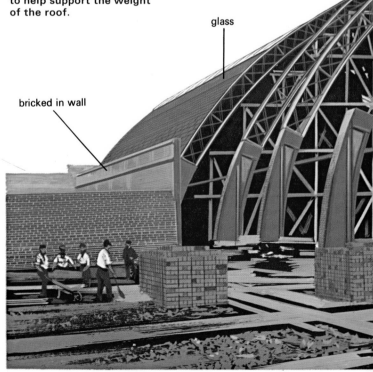

glass

bricked in wall

There is a station at Jamnagar in India which looks as if an English manor house has been set down in the Indian landscape; and the station at Odessa in Russia looks like a cathedral.

Bridges were another important part of railway architecture. Railways had to be carried across valleys and rivers, and the engineers built many-arched viaducts to do this. Railway engineers also introduced new types of iron and steel bridges. One of the most famous of these, and the oldest railway cantilever bridge in the world, is the Forth Bridge in Scotland, with its three large cantilever towers joined by two main spans.

Railway engineers sometimes pioneered new architectural styles and methods of construction, but often they had to compromise and make their buildings fit in with 19th-century ideas about architectural style and design.

▶ **St Pancras Station Hotel (top) and Frankfurt-am-Main Station (below) were built in 19th-century Gothic style.**

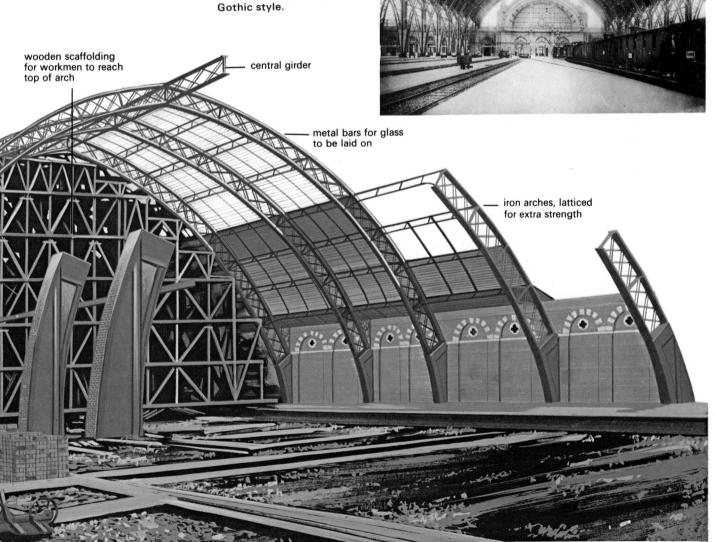

wooden scaffolding for workmen to reach top of arch

central girder

metal bars for glass to be laid on

iron arches, latticed for extra strength

Railways and the people

The railways made it possible for people to travel in a way that had seemed unbelievable a short time before. But what sort of conditions did early railway travellers experience? The first passenger carriages were modelled on the stagecoaches, even – as can be seen in the painting on the right – to the extent of racks on the roof for luggage. Poorer travellers had ridden on the roofs of stagecoaches, but they could not safely ride this way on the roof of railway carriages, so instead there were separate carriages for first, second and third class passengers. Second class carriages were often little more than wooden boxes on wheels with bare seats inside, while third class passengers had at first to travel in open carriages.

Conditions gradually improved. By the 1860s, all carriages were closed in, though often only the first class carriages had padded seats. The carriages were lit by oil lamps. To keep warm, passengers had to rely on thick clothes and footwarmers – metal containers filled with hot water. Travel could still be uncomfortable, and elaborate preparations were needed for a journey by train.

▲ 'The Railway Station' painted by W. P. Frith in 1862 shows the many types of people who travelled by train in Victorian times.

◄ These pictures from 1847 show one artist's view of the three different classes of traveller in the 19th century: the upper classes (top) who had comfortable first class carriages with padded seats and curtained windows; the middle classes (centre) who had to crowd into plain carriages with hard seats; and the working class (bottom) who only had open trucks with wooden planks as seats.

► By 1886 American families travelling west no longer had to go in covered wagons. They could travel from coast to coast by train, on the transcontinental railway. But the journey still took a week, and during that time the train became their home.

The people to whom the railways meant most were the railway workers. They shared a strong bond of unity. In some countries, engine drivers and firemen, signal men and ticket clerks, station masters and porters were the first civilians to wear uniform, and this gave them a sense of importance. Their work on the railway was often hard and uncomfortable. The first engines were not provided with driving cabs, and the guards rode on the tops of the carriages. Pay was not always good, and working hours were long. Yet the railwaymen felt that they were providing a vital service for the people, and they took immense pride in their achievement.

In some countries, the part played by the railways in uniting the people influenced the course of their history. When the railways were first built in Germany, for example, the country was divided into 38 different states. As Germans travelled by train from one state to another, they realized that, although they had differences, they all belonged basically to one nation. A German writer said: 'The frontiers of the races and the states lost their dividing power, rivalries were forgotten, and the Germans discovered the pleasure of getting to know one another.'

The search for comfort: Pullman

As the railways spread across the United States of America, journeys lasting a week or more became common. They were usually very uncomfortable. The travellers had to take their meals hurriedly at station refreshment rooms where the owners often bribed the train drivers to leave early so that food paid for but not eaten could be resold to the next hungry crowd of travellers. At night passengers slept on boards laid across the seats, or in bunk-lined sleeping cars. Only rough mattresses were provided, and the bunks were so close together that a sleeper might wake with someone else's feet in his face.

After enduring these hardships on his journeys, George M. Pullman, a travelling cabinet-maker, decided he would set about designing a carriage in which Americans could 'sleep and eat with more ease and comfort than on a first class steamer!'

In 1863 he built the *Pioneer*. This special carriage had embroidered upholstery and inlaid walnut panels, ornate mirrors and polished brass rails. There were upper berths so the coach could become a sleeping car at night.

At first no railway company would accept the new Pullman car. On every line in the country, station platforms were too wide and bridges too narrow. However, in 1865, George Pullman managed to arrange for the *Pioneer* to be attached to the funeral train which took the body of President Lincoln from Washington to his home town of Springfield in Massachusetts. This railway track had to be adapted to the requirements of the new carriage, and, as a result of the publicity, other railways followed suit. Pullman's improved model, the *Palace* car, was soon adopted by most American transcontinental trains.

In 1866, Pullman built the first dining car; it included everything necessary for a long journey: berths, seats, and, at one end, a kitchen and pantry to provide the meals. He also designed a parlour car with upholstered swivel chairs.

At first Pullman coaches were only used by passengers who could afford to pay a higher fare; but in 1875, railway travel in Britain was transformed when the Midland Railway Company provided upholstered seats in their third class coaches. They abolished the second class, and allowed first class passengers to travel at second class fares. These changes were considered revolutionary because they benefited even the poorest traveller, but they were soon followed by other railway companies.

THESE PALATIAL
PULLMAN HOTEL CARS
ARE RUN BY NO ROAD EXCEPT THE
CHICAGO & NORTH-WESTERN RAILWAY

— BETWEEN —
CHICAGO AND OMAHA

◀ An advertisement shows an early Pullman dining car, first introduced by George Pullman in 1868.

◀ A sleeping car on an American Pullman train of 1882. The passengers' boots are cleaned while they sleep.

▶ This cutaway shows a 19th-century Pullman coach with sleeping berths, inlaid panels and upholstered seats.
   At night the bunks, concealed behind the sloping panels above the windows of the carriage, were let down to make it a sleeping car.

Cars like this, with their floor carpets, elaborate decoration and many oil lamps were the last word in in 19th-century luxury travel.

► A poster of 1876 advertises the Great Western Route from New York and Boston to Chicago and San Francisco. The entire journey was made in Pullman cars.

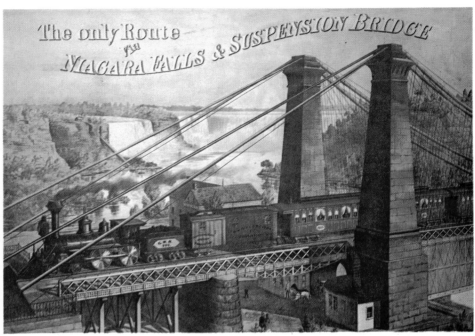

◄ Pullman coaches in Europe. A poster for the 1929 Paris-Brussels-Amsterdam Express shows passengers travelling in comfort.

The Orient Express

In Europe, unlike America, a long distance train had to cross national boundaries. In 1876, Georges Nagelmackers, a Belgian engineer, founded an international company which created something quite new in rail travel: the Orient Express, an international train operated by an individual promoter, and crossing the boundaries of many different countries.

On the evening of 4 October 1883, a small group of diplomats, officials and journalists assembled in the Gare de l'Est in Paris for the first journey of the Orient Express across Central Europe to Constantinople (modern Istanbul). The train was different from anything they had seen before. Each passenger coach was divided into two compartments furnished with red plush armchairs, Turkish carpets and inlaid tables, while the silk-covered walls could be folded down at night to make deeply upholstered beds. There was a bathroom with hot and cold water, a smoking room and a servants' dormitory.

The train ran smoothly – Nagelmackers had copied the American way of mounting the coaches on pivoted undercarriages (bogies) instead of on 2 or 3 axles. The passengers dined in a restaurant car, which was lined with tapestries and had a ceiling decorated with embossed leather. The 5-course dinner lasted for 3 hours.

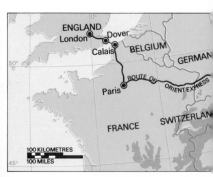

▲ The route of the Orient Express. It crossed many national boundaries, and ushered in a new era of international travel.

◄ Menus on the Orient Express included exotic dishes from the countries through which the train passed.

▼ A music hall poster from the late 19th century makes fun of night life on board the Orient Express. Since its first journey the Orient Express has captured popular imagination.

The Orient Express was faster than other trains because no halts were made for food or sleep; moreover the passengers' luggage was stored in a sealed van so that only hand baggage had to be checked by customs officers at each border, and this was usually done while the train was on the move. The journey from Paris to Constantinople took only 67½ hours. But it was not cheap. A return ticket for 2 people and a servant cost £160 in 1885, which was about the same as a year's rent on a large fashionable house. Yet there were people wealthy enough to afford this and to enjoy the experience of taking a romantic journey on the world's first great international train.

▲ A still from the film of Agatha Christie's book, *Murder on the Orient Express*. The Orient Express also inspired the author, Graham Greene, to write *Stamboul Train*, a thriller in which all the action takes place on a journey from Paris to Istanbul.

▼ This film poster shows a sinister Hercule Poirot – played by Albert Finney – waiting for the train to leave. Many international stars took part in the film, capturing the exotic atmosphere which has always been associated with the Orient Express.

AGATHA CHRISTIE's
Murder on the Orient Express

ALBERT FINNEY · LAUREN BACALL · MARTIN BALSAM · INGRID BERGMAN · JACQUELINE BISSET · JEAN-PIERRE CASSEL · SEAN CONNERY · JOHN GIELGUD · WENDY HILLER · ANTHONY PERKINS · VANESSA REDGRAVE · RACHEL ROBERTS · RICHARD WIDMARK · MICHAEL YORK with COLIN BLAKELY · GEORGE COULOURIS · DENIS QUILLEY

MUSIC COMPOSED BY RICHARD RODNEY BENNETT · SCREENPLAY BY PAUL DEHN · PRODUCED BY JOHN BRABOURNE & RICHARD GOODWIN · DIRECTED BY SIDNEY LUMET EMI

Railways and leisure

◄ Three posters advertising excursion trains. The 'Excursion Train Galop' (left) was a lively dance tune published in 1862. The poster from France (centre) shows the comfort and convenience provided by the dining car. Skegness (right) was a popular seaside resort in the 1900s.

▼ A jokey look at some of the different types of people who went on holiday by train. You can tell by their clothes and luggage the sort of holiday each of them is expecting!

Until the middle of the 19th century very few people were able to go away for even a short holiday. This was changed by the coming of the railways, and especially by the organization of excursion trains which took people away for a day trip at a reduced rate.

The first excursion train was run in England in 1840. Members of the Nottingham Mechanics' Institute wanted to visit an exhibition at Leicester. When the railway company heard this, they decided to run a special train charging only half-fares. This inspired Thomas Cook, a local printer, to persuade the railway company the next year to run an excursion train for 570 passengers from Leicester to Loughborough. This was the first publicly advertised railway excursion. The fare was a shilling. It was so successful that Thomas Cook continued to organize similar trips and founded a travel firm which still operates all over the world.

The early railway excursions were such a novelty that the passengers were treated like conquering heroes. They marched to the station to the music of a band and were greeted by it on their return.

The favourite places for 19th-century railway excursionists were the seaside resorts. The first seaside place in England to become a popular holiday town was Brighton, following the opening of the railway from London in 1841.

In France railway excursions were arranged from Paris to Dieppe, Boulogne and other places on the Channel coast. Early French excursion trains were often just cattle trucks fitted with wooden seats. On one journey, when a ticket collector entered the truck, the travellers greeted him with loud cries of 'Moo! Moo!'; and when the train stopped at the station, they lowered their heads and, still bellowing vigorously, charged through the gate which led from the station to the cattle yard, while the railway staff stood by laughing helplessly. Very soon afterwards, carriages were introduced for all journeys on that particular line!

Excursions were arranged in much the same way in all countries. Sometimes a whole train was hired by a firm for its workers, or by a church or society; but generally the trip was organized by the railway company, which sold the tickets at greatly reduced prices. The excursions were held on traditional holidays such as Easter and Whitsun and on Sundays, the only days on which most people did not have to work in their factories, shops or offices.

Special trains were organized for all sorts of people: ramblers in the countryside, spectators at football matches, and racegoers. For many people such trains were the only way they could hope to get away from the town or village where they lived and worked to enjoy a day in a different environment.

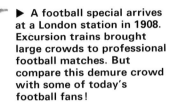

▶ A football special arrives at a London station in 1908. Excursion trains brought large crowds to professional football matches. But compare this demure crowd with some of today's football fans!

▼ Modern French excursionists descend from their train ready to enjoy a summer holiday at the seaside. Many people today still travel on holiday by train.

The Blue Train

◀ An attraction for visitors to Monte Carlo was the La Turbie restaurant and hotel. It was 460 metres above the sea and could be reached by a cog-wheel railway from Monte Carlo.

SUMMER ON THE FRENCH RIVIERA BY THE BLUE TRAIN

▲ A poster advertises the delights of the French Riviera, which can be reached by the Blue Train.

▶ The Blue Train reaches Nice. The elegant passengers wait among the palm trees at the station for their luggage to be taken to luxurious Riviera hotels. Only the rich could afford to holiday here.

In December 1883, only three months after the first Orient Express made the journey from Paris to Constantinople, Georges Nagelmackers started another international train. The Calais-Mediterranean went from Paris to Marseilles and then continued along the Riviera to Nice. It was even more luxurious than the Orient Express. Only 10 people travelled in each coach, under the care of a servant-valet employed by the railway company. Even the corridor was completely carpeted, and the train contained the first travelling cocktail bar and a 'Pergola Restaurant'.

This train became very popular among the upper classes of Europe who discovered for the first time the beautiful scenery and superb climate of the Riviera. The South of France has milder winters than anywhere else in Europe, and it soon became fashionable to spend the cold and disagreeable winter months in comfort on the French Riviera.

Every autumn English aristocrats, Russian and German princes and princesses, American millionaires and their families, arrived at the station in Paris and were installed in their luxurious private compartments. On the platform, porters struggled with the baggage, railwaymen tested the couplings of the carriages, and the train's chef supervised the last-minute delivery of blocks of ice and fresh vegetables for his kitchen.

Once the train had left Paris, the passengers began to change for dinner, and soon an attendant walked down the corridor ringing a bell to summon them to the Pergola Restaurant. After the 5-course meal, the passengers found that the attendants had made up their beds. As they slept, the train sped southwards through the night to reach the Mediterranean coast early in the morning. At Marseilles when they woke passengers had their first view of the gently rising hills and bright blue sea.

At Nice the passengers were met by interpreters of every nationality and by liveried coachmen from the hotels. Aristocrats and their bejewelled wives, impeccable young men and elegant young ladies, were whisked away to their hotels.

Many of the wealthiest and smartest of the train's passengers, however, did not stay at Nice. They went on to the gambling casino at Monte Carlo in the tiny principality of Monaco. Each year hundreds of gamblers went to 'Monte' which acquired a reputation as a place for reckless enjoyment.

After World War I, the Mediterranean Express resumed its interrupted service and the train's livery was changed from varnished teak to dark blue. The Express became known as the 'Blue Train' to all its passengers; although it was only in 1949 that the Wagons-Lits Company changed the destination plaque on the carriages so that the train was officially given the name by which it had been known for years.

Royal trains

In 1842, only four years after the first section of the Great Western Railway, from London to Maidenhead, had been completed, Queen Victoria went from Slough to Paddington in a saloon fitted with crimson and white silk hangings, fine paintings and sofas of carved wood. Brunel himself travelled on the foot plate of the engine. The Queen was so pleased with the journey that she travelled frequently by train for the rest of her reign. The railway companies built complete royal trains for her, with carriages containing drawing-rooms, dining-rooms, bathrooms and kitchens. Queen Victoria insisted that a royal train must never be driven at more than 40 mph (64 kph), and in 1850 her Secretary wrote complaining that she had been in a train driven at the unholy rate of 60 mph (96 kph)! In contrast to this, the most recent British royal train, built for Queen Elizabeth II for the Silver Jubilee celebrations in 1977, was designed to run at up to 160 kilometres an hour.

The British royal family often travelled by train in other countries. The French railway kept a pair of special saloons at Calais which Queen Victoria used whenever she went to the Riviera. In 1900, her son, the future King Edward VII, was the object of an assassination attempt at Brussels station. A student fired a pistol at him through the open window of his carriage. The bullet hit the panelling and the Prince joked about his would-be assassin's bad marksmanship as he ordered the train to proceed.

King Wilhelm I of Prussia was a soldier and preferred to travel simply. His train consisted only of a plain day saloon, study and 'sleeping-chamber' which contained his favourite camp bed.

Napoleon III of France, on the other hand, had a royal express with nine richly-appointed carriages, a wine cellar and a conservatory of flowers. Tsar Alexander III of Russia bought this train, enlarged it to 15 carriages and added fittings which made it the costliest train in the world. There was a playroom and a night nursery for the imperial children, and even a cow car containing two Holstein cows to provide milk. The Tsar was so afraid of assassination that when the imperial train passed through the countryside, all other trains had to wait in sidings with their windows closed, their doors locked and with a sentry standing guard by each carriage.

▲ Queen Victoria and King Louis Philippe descend from the royal train during an official visit to England by the French king. Notice the flags draped above the station.

▼ One of the imperial trains belonging to Napoleon III, Emperor of France, 1852–70. It had carriages for all his aides, and a special gilded viewing carriage for the emperor.

▲ The highly ornate engine of a train used by one of the viceroys of Egypt during the 19th century.

Even more magnificent was the yellow 16-coach train of Tz'u-Hsi, the 'Dragon Empress' who ruled China from 1861 to 1908. Two coaches were set aside as kitchens to prepare 100-course dinners. Her 40 pairs of shoes and 2,000 gowns required a carriage to themselves. Her bedroom contained a huge bed of polished teak, and the windows were curtained with yellow silk. The carriage which contained her throne was fitted out to resemble as closely as possible the throne room in her imperial palace at Peking. She always insisted that important railway officials travelled with her so that she could order their immediate execution if anything went wrong.

▶ The interior of the saloon carriage built for Queen Victoria by the London and North Western Railway in 1869. It is probably the most luxurious royal carriage ever built. The ceiling and walls are covered with silk quilting. The noise of the train is deadened by a double floor filled in with cork and covered with a thick overlay of felt and a deep-pile carpet.

Opening up the world

During the 19th century, engineers built railway lines which opened up entire continents to travel and to trade.

Railway engineers in the Andes in South America built lines at greater heights than anywhere else in the world, and they had to protect them from the constant threat of avalanches and snowdrifts. One of the most remarkable lines was built from Callao into the mountains of Peru, Chile and Bolivia. On one stretch of over 160 kilometres, the engineers had to provide 21 reversing stations, where the train, having no space to turn at the end of one climb, could back towards the next stage of its ascent. The train also had to pass through long tunnels before it reached its final height of over 4,500 metres. Oxygen was carried to revive passengers who felt faint because of the thin air at this great height.

▲ A scene at the railway station in Lagos, Nigeria, in the early 1920s. The railway helped to bring unity to Nigeria.

▶ Passengers and their belongings crowd into a train during a halt on the Yunnan Railway in south-western China in 1925.

The distance from Port Pirie to Kalgoorlie in Australia is 1,783 kilometres, but there were few natural obstacles to railway construction, so, on this Trans-Australia line, tunnels and bridges were not needed. The railway was completed within 5 years. The line across the Nullabor Plain is the longest straight stretch of railway track in the world: a section of 497 kilometres without a single curve. Water supply was the worst problem; it had to be carried over 500 kilometres by special wagons.

The first railway in China was built by British merchants near Shanghai in 1875, but the steaming monsters caused such alarm that some mandarins came by sedan chair from Peking with sacks of money, bought the entire railway and at once dismantled it. It was 20 years before the Chinese began to build their own railways.

In 19th-century Africa, there were plans to build a great north-to-south railway from Cairo to the Cape, but this was never completed. Instead, the colonial powers concentrated on building lines within their own territories. The line built in 1900 in the Gold Coast (now Ghana) was typical. It linked the gold mines near Tarkwa with the coast, 65 kilometres away. The line passed through hot, wet tropical jungle where the wooden pegs driven into the ground to mark the route sprouted into small trees and had to be replaced with concrete blocks. The construction was brought to a halt when Ashanti tribesmen attacked the surveyors and engineers and forced them to retreat to the coast. They were besieged for nearly four months, until a British force relieved them. Within a year, the first train was taking a load of heavy mining machinery to Tarkwa.

◄ The isolated station of Tres Marias in Mexico, 1901. It is the village's only link with the outside world.

► President Nyerere of Tanzania and President Kaunda of Zambia attend a track-laying ceremony near the border town of Tunduma to mark the completion, in 1973, of the Tanzam Railway linking their countries. The railway was planned and financed by the Chinese, who hoped thereby to increase their influence in Africa.

▼ A modern South American train climbs a lofty valley in the mountains of Peru.

▼ The Mauritania railway on a lonely stretch of line between Char and Zouerate.

▲ A locomotive of the Indian Southern Railway. The Indian railway system was planned and built by the British in the 19th century.

Journey on an Indian train

By the opening years of the 20th century, the British had built in India one of the largest railway systems in the world, and European travellers began to go on sightseeing tours around the sub-continent. The journey often began at Victoria Terminus in Bombay, a massive station built in a Gothic style with arches, columns and stained glass. From here ran such famous expresses as the Blue Train to Calcutta, the Deccan Queen to Poona, and the Frontier Mail to Delhi and the north.

Europeans travelled first class, usually four to a compartment containing two armchairs, a table, a chest of drawers and two sofas running lengthwise. There were two upper berths, which were folded away during the day. The traveller had to provide his own bedding in the form of a 'bed-bag', which was a large canvas bag containing a rolled-up mattress, sheets, pillows and blankets. Although the expresses had restaurant cars and there were refreshment rooms at most stations, few travellers left Bombay without a tiffin-box containing a teapot, cups and saucers, plates and spoons, a tin of biscuits, a pot of marmalade and all the necessaries for a snack.

▶ 19th-century European travellers hired Indian servants at the railway station. The servants travelled in a special compartment and looked after the European sahib and his luggage.

▼ Travelling by train in 19th-century India could be very pleasant if the weather was not too hot, and if the traveller had a water pipe to smoke and servants to brew his tea and take care of his luggage.

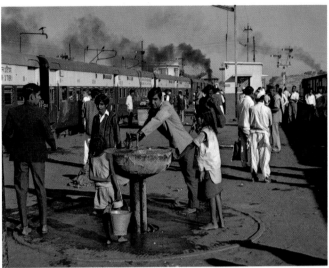

▲ The busy platform at Mehsana junction in central India. Indian stations are a hive of activity, and often a commercial and business centre as well.

▼ Eager travellers perch on the engine itself on this mountain railway in Darjeeling. It is one of the world's most famous small railways.

In some ways first class railway travel in India was the most comfortable in the world, but it had its disadvantages. In the summer months, the heat was so intense that fans brought no relief. Servants bought large blocks of ice at the stations which were placed in special containers on the floor of the compartment in an effort to bring the temperature down. Sometimes matting was fixed outside the windows. This was kept damp and helped to cool the air blowing into the compartment.

In the monsoon season, engine drivers had to keep a special watch on stretches of the track liable to flood. These were indicated by black and white posts marked with a bright red crossbar. If this bar was submerged the water was so deep that it would extinguish the engine's fire, so the train had to stop where it was until the waters had subsided.

Railway stations in India were social centres and bazaars, where almost everything was sold. People might wait two or three days for their train, eating, sleeping and washing on the platforms. When the train came in there was a rush for the third class carriages which could hold as many as 120 people. Sometimes a beggar, invariably without a ticket, was pulled off by railway police. As the train left the station it passed gangs of convicts repairing the rails and poor people picking cinders from the track.

In hilly country where there were great loops in the line, passengers could stretch their legs by leaving the slowly climbing train and walking across the loop at a leisurely pace until they rejoined the train on the next section of the ascent.

The Trans-Siberian railway

In 1891 the Tsar of Russia with great ceremony laid the foundation stone of a railway which was to cross the vast Russian empire from Moscow to Vladivostock, a distance of nearly 10,000 kilometres. It was to provide the first overland link between Western Europe and the Far East. The construction of this line took ten years to complete.

Foreign engineers were not impressed by the Russian achievement. The railway was single track for its whole length. Three-quarters of the bridges were made of wood. In the depths of winter, rails were laid across frozen land which became water-logged in the summer. Towns had to bribe officials to get the line to pass through them.

When the line was complete it was used by two Trans-Siberian expresses. One was run by the Russian Imperial Government. It consisted of three carriages, one first class and two second class, and a vehicle containing a dining room, kitchen, bathroom and luggage section; sometimes, for third class passengers, it also had a goods van fitted with bunks but without washing or cooking facilities.

The other Trans-Siberian Express provided a complete contrast. It was a luxurious train supplied by Georges Nagelmackers, who had built the Orient Express. Each coach accommodated only eight people and had its own drawing room and smoking room. The dining room served delicious and elegant meals.

▼ Map showing the route of the Trans-Siberian railway. Notice the immense size of the country it had to cover, which stretches from northern Europe right across to China. Notice also the difficulties the railway builders had to face, with the cold and the mountains.

◄ ▶ Building the Trans-Siberian railway. Many engineers in the West criticised the way the railway was built, but often they did not take into account the immense obstacles which the Russian engineers had to overcome in its construction.

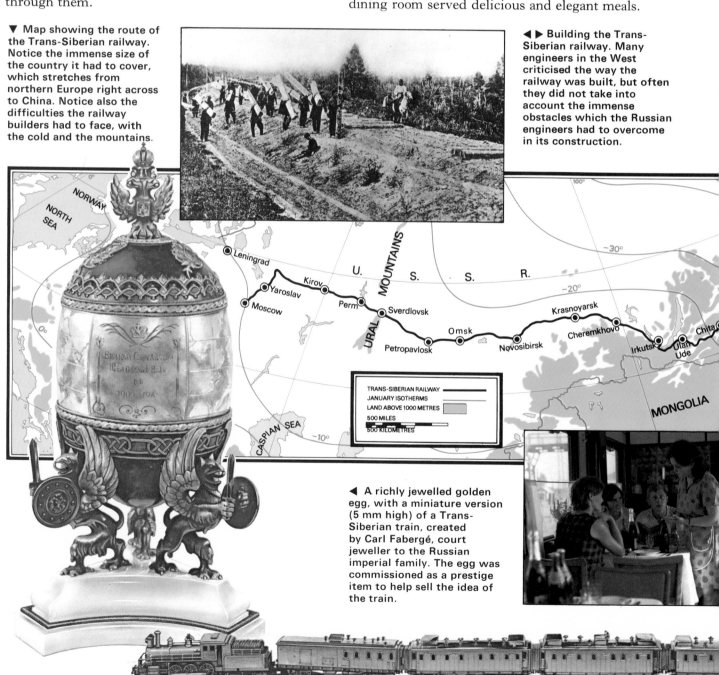

◄ A richly jewelled golden egg, with a miniature version (5 mm high) of a Trans-Siberian train, created by Carl Fabergé, court jeweller to the Russian imperial family. The egg was commissioned as a prestige item to help sell the idea of the train.

The lucky passengers on the Nagelmackers train made the journey from Moscow to Vladivostock in nine days. Even for them, however, the journey was seldom without incident. There was a gap in the line at Lake Baikal, across which the passengers were transported by boat. In the depths of winter, when the lake was frozen over, the train travelled across the ice; in 1904 a locomotive plunged through a crack and was lost. Soon afterwards, the line around the south of the lake was completed.

An Englishman who travelled on the Trans-Siberian in the autumn of 1902 described the intense cold encountered in Siberia. He noted: 'We were stopped for a few minutes; I got out and ran up and down for exercise, but found the cold so great that I was glad to get on board again, for fear of having my ears frost-bitten, they having become perfectly numb.' He was also rather doubtful about the condition of the line: 'The railway in its entirety is flimsy and liable to collapse almost everywhere, and I am certain it could never sustain a large volume of heavy traffic.'

His words were to be proved true. When Russia went to war against Japan in 1905, the line was quite unable to meet Russia's military needs. Trains were derailed and vital supplies delayed all along the route. The bad condition of the Trans-Siberian railway contributed towards the overwhelming Russian defeat by Japan.

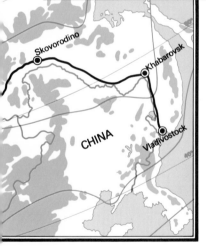

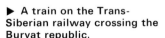
◀ A dining car on a modern Trans-Siberian Express. The train today serves as an important link across the vast expanse of the Soviet Union.

▶ A train on the Trans-Siberian railway crossing the Buryat republic.

Railways in Japan

▲ American sailors from Commodore Perry's fleet demonstrate their model railway to the Japanese during their visit to Yokohama in March 1854.

▼ A Japanese artist's impression of the scene at the opening, in the presence of the Emperor, of the first railway in Japan at Tokyo in 1872.

Until the middle of the 19th century, the Japanese had little contact with foreigners and followed their traditional way of life. Their seclusion was brought to an end one day in July 1853 when four American warships anchored off the Japanese coast. They were commanded by Commodore Matthew Perry who had been sent by his government to open up trade with Japan. The warships were the first steamships most Japanese people had ever seen. The local officials were alarmed at the sight, but they promised to deliver a message from the President of the United States to the Emperor of Japan.

When Perry returned eight months later, he brought with him a miniature steam locomotive. The American sailors set it up on shore, and it drew a train of small carriages. The Japanese crowded round and tried to ride on it. The carriages were too small for them to get into, so they sat on the roof, clinging to the edge as the train steamed along its track, their long silk robes flapping in the wind. They themselves were both amused and afraid at this new experience which heralded the start of another age.

▶ The bullet train on the new Tokaido line, passing Mount Fuji. It travels between Tokyo and Yokohama at an average speed of 160 kilometres an hour.

▼ Crowds on the platform during the Tokyo rush hour. Special porters help to push passengers into the carriage.

It was nearly 20 years, however, before Japan actually built its first railway. In 1872 there was a rice famine in an outlying part of the country. Because it was so difficult to transport relief supplies, the government decided that the country must have a railway system. The first line, which was built by British engineers, was 29 kilometres long and linked Tokyo with Yokohama.

The Japanese found it difficult to get used to the new way of travel. It was the traditional custom in Japan, for instance, to leave one's shoes outside the door when entering a house, and sometimes early Japanese travellers did the same when they went on a train and watched with dismay as the train pulled out of the station, leaving their shoes carefully arranged in a neat row on the platform. Japanese ladies were anxious that their elaborate hair-styles should not suffer during long train journeys, so the railway company provided a device called a *makura* on which they could rest their neck at night without disarranging their hair.

With the railway came the telegraph, and at first the Japanese were amazed by this: in the countryside, people watched the telegraph wires expecting to be able to see the messages travel along them from station to station.

By the beginning of the 20th century, however, the Japanese had accepted the railway as part of their way of life, and had a system that rivalled those in most other countries. Between 1959 and 1962, a new line was built on which 'bullet trains' reached speeds of 250 kilometres an hour. These high speed trains are today among the most efficient and up-to-date in the world.

The Canadian Pacific

In 1867 most of the British colonies in North America united to form the Dominion of Canada. However the most westerly of them, British Columbia, refused to join until 1871, and then only on condition that a transcontinental railway were begun within ten years. In 1881 the Canadian Pacific Railway Company began the construction of the line from Montreal to Vancouver in British Columbia, a distance of nearly 5,000 kilometres.

The difficulties were immense. Some years before, a surveyor looking for a possible route had reported: 'The knowledge of the country as a whole would never lead me to advocate a line of communication across the continent to the Pacific.'

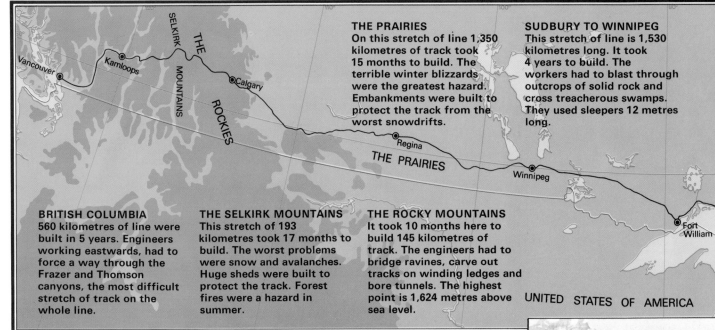

THE PRAIRIES
On this stretch of line 1,350 kilometres of track took 15 months to build. The terrible winter blizzards were the greatest hazard. Embankments were built to protect the track from the worst snowdrifts.

SUDBURY TO WINNIPEG
This stretch of line is 1,530 kilometres long. It took 4 years to build. The workers had to blast through outcrops of solid rock and cross treacherous swamps. They used sleepers 12 metres long.

BRITISH COLUMBIA
560 kilometres of line were built in 5 years. Engineers working eastwards, had to force a way through the Frazer and Thomson canyons, the most difficult stretch of track on the whole line.

THE SELKIRK MOUNTAINS
This stretch of 193 kilometres took 17 months to build. The worst problems were snow and avalanches. Huge sheds were built to protect the track. Forest fires were a hazard in summer.

THE ROCKY MOUNTAINS
It took 10 months here to build 145 kilometres of track. The engineers had to bridge ravines, carve out tracks on winding ledges and bore tunnels. The highest point is 1,624 metres above sea level.

◀ An engineers' camp in the Selkirk Mountains during the construction of the Canadian Pacific Railway.

◀ **Part of the Canadian Pacific Railway in 1886. Mountain ravines were crossed by massive wooden trestle viaducts made from timber cut in the nearby forests.**

▶ **A modern Canadian Pacific train crosses a viaduct in the Rocky Mountains. The train is provided with a view-dome so that passengers can admire the breathtaking scenery.**

The route of the Canadian Pacific Railway.

MONTREAL TO SUDBURY This part of the line is 708 kilometres long. It had already been built in 1881, when the Canadian Pacific Company was formed, and they bought it as the first stretch of their new railway line.

C A N A D A

| LAND ABOVE 1000 METRES |
| INTERNATIONAL BOUNDARY |
| ROUTE OF CANADIAN PACIFIC RAILWAY |
| 100 MILES |
| 100 KILOMETRES |

Sudbury

Montreal

◀ **This photograph, taken in 1883, shows the railway being built through the Rocky Mountains.**

▼ **Passengers in a tourist sleeping car during the early days of the Canadian Pacific Railway.**

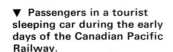

It took four years to build 320 kilometres of railway across the swamps north of Lake Superior. It needed 12,000 men, 2,000 teams of horses and 12 ships for the transport of material and provisions. Tons of explosives blasted through solid rock, and the rails could only be kept in place across the swamps by laying them on sleepers 12 metres long.

There were fewer obstacles in prairie country and over 1,300 kilometres were laid in 15 months. The men worked in 5-hour shifts during the freezing winter, wearing large gauntlets to shield their hands from frostbite, and woollen socks over their high leather boots to prevent them slipping on the ice. They lived in tented camps, and their food consisted mainly of oatmeal, pork, beans and bannocks.

After the prairies came the immense mountain barriers of the Rockies and the Selkirks, where 340 kilometres of track took 27 months to build. Gangs of workers built eastwards from the Pacific to meet the builders advancing westwards. They blasted cuttings through solid rock, and bored tunnels, including an 8-kilometre tunnel under Mount Macdonald. They crossed mountain ravines with great wooden trestle viaducts. There were new inventions to help the builders: powerful dynamite charges for blasting, and steam shovels which shifted crushed rocks and other debris. Without these, the earlier surveyor might have been right in his prediction that a transcontinental line could not be built.

Finally in 1885 the eastern and western tracks met in the Selkirks and a ceremonial last spike was driven in. The line was complete, and the western seaboard of Canada was united at last with the rest of the country.

Unusual railways

The history of railways is full of all sorts of oddities. Trains have had to perform unusual tasks and meet unusual conditions.

Mountains provide railways with some of the most difficult problems: when gradients are steeper than one in 14, ordinary locomotive wheels cannot grip the rails. One solution is the rack or log railway, which is widely used in Switzerland. The locomotives have a toothed wheel which grips a rack laid alongside the track. Another railway which can climb steep gradients is the funicular, or cable railway. Thick cables pass round the huge wheel of a winding-engine and are connected to two cars running on rails. As one car goes up the slope, the other comes down, controlled by the cable passing over rollers in the middle of the track. In this way, the weight of the ascending car is balanced by that of the descending car. If the car going downhill needs more weight, water ballast is put in its special tank and gradually released as it goes down. Near Santos, in Brazil, complete trains are split into sections, each of which is drawn up the mountain in turn by cable. When all the carriages have reached the top, they are joined up again.

Other unusual railways are narrow-gauge systems. These have sometimes been built to open up backward regions. In the hilly districts of India, for example, there are tracks which are only 61 centimetres wide. The railway at the Guinness Brewery in Dublin also has a narrow track with a gauge of only 56 centimetres. It was built in 1878 on two levels connected by a steep spiral tunnel. The small steam engines which were originally used on the railway had their cylinders mounted above the boiler to keep the working parts clean.

▲ Three examples of climbing railways: (left) the Vitnam-Righi railway in Switzerland; (centre) the cable railway linking Zurich's university with the town; (right) the Snowdon mountain railway in Wales

▼ An artist's impression of a railway that never was: the Tehuantepec Railway in Mexico that was planned to pull ships from the Atlantic to the Pacific Ocean. Today this is done by the Panama Canal.

In the 1890s, when there was no canal linking the Atlantic with the Pacific Ocean, there were plans to build a unique railway across the Isthmus of Tehuantepec in Mexico. At each end of the line, powerful steam winches would lift cargo from the ships and place it on goods trains. These would take the cargo across the isthmus. Small ships could be lifted out of the water and pulled by train from one sea to the other.

This line was made unnecessary by the completion of the Panama Canal in 1915. But an unusual railway was built on both sides of the Panama Canal. Electric motors, which were called 'mules', hauled the ships through the locks. At the end of each lock, the locomotive climbed up a steep incline to reach the higher level. A large ship needed as many as twelve locomotives to haul it up.

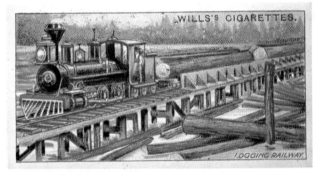

Railways in all their variety have formed a popular theme for cigarette cards (as here), stamps, matchbox covers and many other collectors' items. Why not start collecting them?

▲ A logging railway in Canada is illustrated on a cigarette card.

▼ Another cigarette card shows a rotary snow-plough on the Swedish State Railways.

▲ A narrow-gauge engine drawing empty casks to the cleansing area at the Guinness Brewery in Dublin, 1930.

▼ A miniature steam engine on the Romney, Hythe and Dymchurch Railway, which is popular with holidaymakers.

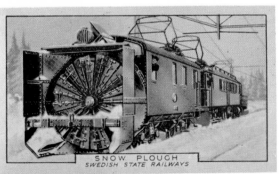

Trains in cities

Underground railways were first built in the later part of the 19th century as an answer to the problems presented by the rapid growth of great cities and the slowness of horse traffic in their streets. The building of lines beneath the city streets was expensive, but the trains were fast and when they were eventually electrified, did not add more smoke to the already polluted atmosphere.

The first underground railway in the world was the Metropolitan Railway, which was opened between Paddington and Farringdon Street in London in 1863. It was followed in 1868 by the first section of the District Railway between Kensington and Westminster. Both of these lines, and the later extensions to them, were built mainly by the 'cut-and-cover' method – digging a trench for the railway and then roofing it over. Both lines used steam engines, which condensed their steam in special side tanks, but filled the tunnels with dirty, choking clouds of sulphurous smoke.

The first 'tube' railway, constructed by boring through the earth from underground working sites, was the City and South London Railway. The line was opened in 1890, and was the first railway to have electric trains.

▲ A suburban train passing over a level crossing in Paris, 1885. Trains travelling above ground caused congestion and delay in large cities during the 19th century.

▼ One answer to the problem was the elevated railway. Here is the first one in America being tested in 1867.

In 19th-century America, several cities solved their transport difficulties by constructing elevated railways, which ran on trestles over the streets. These were cheaper and easier to build than underground railways, but the trains spread smoke, cinders and noise, frightened horses and shook buildings as they went by. They were, however, fast, and the fares were low. They became a popular means of travel, especially in New York, where one critical citizen said: 'People are packed in their cars like sardines in a box with perspiration for oil.'

The Paris Metro, an electrified underground railway, was built in 1900, using the cut-and-cover method of construction. The underground in Moscow is perhaps the most beautiful in the world. The walls and pillars of its stations are covered with white, black and pink marble, and artificial light is supplied through a roof of coloured glass. Rotterdam, which rests upon water-logged peat and clay, built its underground railway by digging upon channels and sinking into the water pre-cast concrete sections, which are sealed together to hold the lines.

▲ Farringdon Road Station on the Metropolitan Railway in 1868. The first underground lines in London were built in deep trenches and later arched over.

▶ A scene on the elevated railway in New York during the 1890s. Despite reports, the horses here do not seem afraid of the steam engines.

◀ The interior of the recently modernized Louvre Station on the Paris Métro. Full-size casts of Egyptian and Greek sculptures stand in lighted niches along the platforms of the underground station.

▲ A modern elevated railway in Wuppertal, Germany. This is a monorail in which the passenger cars are suspended below a single rail. The monorail is often cheaper to run and faster than other railways.

Railways in war

The first war in which railways played in important military role was the American Civil War (1860-65). Without the railway, the Union forces could not have waged the victorious campaigns which took them nearly 500 kilometres from their bases. When General Sherman made his astonishing march from Chattanooga down into Georgia he was supplied only by a single line of railway passing through hostile territory. The Southern Confederate forces constantly attacked it, ripping up rails and burning the sleepers, but the trains were never stopped for more than a day.

In 1862, 21 Northern Federal soldiers seized the Confederate locomotive, *General*, from Kenneshaw in Georgia. They intended to steam up the line to Chattanooga, nearly 160 kilometres away, blowing up tunnels and burning bridges. A determined Confederate engineman chased them in another locomotive, the *Texas*, keeping so close that the Federals could not stop to damage the line or refuel the *General*. The two locomotives raced along at over 95 km an hour. 32 kilometres from Chattanooga the *General* ran out of fuel. The Federal soldiers tried to escape through the forest but were captured.

The railway was used as a weapon during the Boer War in Southern Africa (1899–1902). The British patrolled the countryside with armoured trains. These protected isolated British outposts, but they were always in danger of being derailed by Boer commandos.

In 1862, during the American Civil War, some Federal soldiers drove away the Confederate locomotive, *General*, in Georgia. They were chased by Confederate railwaymen in another engine, the *Texas*, which kept so close to them that they could neither refuel their engine nor carry out their plan of damaging the line as they went. The two engines raced along at 100 kilometres an hour until the *General* ran out of fuel.

The *Texas*

The *General*

▲ (Left) An early British armoured train in Egypt during the Sudan War, 1881.

(Right) British troops, returning from leave, about to board the boat train at Victoria Station, London, on their way back to France during World War I.

◄ A German supply train in France, damaged by Allied bombers during World War II.

▼ Russian soldiers take cover behind a train during fighting at a railway station in the area of Lvov in the Ukraine, 1944, when the Russian army was taking the offensive against the German invaders. During their retreat, the German forces tried to destroy the railways to impede Russian progress.

In World War I both sides moved troops and wounded men, munitions and supplies by trains that ran as near to the front as possible despite constant enemy shelling from artillery behind the lines.

During World War II the Allies prepared for the German invasion of France in 1944 by bombing the French railways, destroying vital junctions, bridges and goods yards. When the Allied troops landed, the French Resistance went into action, sabotaging locomotives, damaging signals, blowing up sections of the track and attacking trains. The Germans could not move enough men and supplies by train and had to resort to convoys of road vehicles.

The Germans destroyed railway lines as they retreated from France and Russia so that they could not be used by the Allies. They mounted a steel hook on an open truck which tore up the track behind it as it was pulled along by a locomotive.

Competition for the railways

By the middle of the 19th century, railways were the most important form of transport in many parts of the world. They remained the most important until after World War I. Even before 1914, however, competition began to appear from city tramways.

The first tramway was built between New York and Harlem in 1832. Its passenger tramcars became the cheapest form of transport in Manhattan. Tramways were introduced into France in 1855, England in 1860, and then into towns all over the world. The early trams were horse-drawn. Steam locomotives for tramcars were first developed in England in 1872 and became widely used. Tramcars became most successful, however, after they started to use electric power in the 1890s. During the early years of the 20th century, the electric tramcar, because of its more frequent service and lower fares, captured much of the short-distance suburban railway traffic in large cities.

▲ The first challenge to the railways came from the tramways in the middle of the 19th century. The illustration at the top, dating from the 1890s, shows the older horse trams and the new electric trams working alongside each other.

▲ An early Daimler car, 1908. The most severe challenge to the railways began with the invention of the petrol engine.

▼ The Wright brothers make the first successful flight by aeroplane in 1903, and start a whole new era in transport.

The tramways enjoyed only a brief triumph. Already a new form of transport was being developed which would undermine both tramcars and railways. During the 1880s the internal combustion engine, using petrol as a fuel, was developed in Germany and France. Soon there were petrol-driven vehicles on the roads of Europe and America. In 1908 Henry Ford began to build the Model T, the world's first cheap, mass-produced car.

From 1920 onwards the motor vehicle made rapid progress. It affected the railways in many ways. Motor buses became the most common form of passenger transport in towns. Motor coaches often proved to be cheaper for long distance journeys and were not restricted in their routes by having to run on tracks. The increasing use of the private motor car gave more people the freedom to go where they chose. At the same time long distance road haulage was taking much of the goods traffic away from the railways.

The railways also faced a challenge from another competitor, one which could achieve greater speeds than they could hope to attain – the aeroplane. By the second half of the 20th century, it had become, all over the world, a serious rival on both long and short journeys. Many people now travel by plane rather than by train, whether on holiday or for business. The result is that everywhere countries have reduced the great networks of railway lines which were built in the 19th century.

The railways of today save money and operate more efficiently by running frequent fast trains for both passengers and goods between larger towns and cities. These trains are mostly electric or diesel powered, and are cheaper and more efficient than the steam train. The steam locomotive which dominated the railway age has largely disappeared from railways all over the world.

▲ Heavy traffic on a motorway in Austria. In the last century the coming of the railways led to roads being neglected. Today it is the other way round. Roads are taking the traffic away from the railways. This is not always a good thing, and often the countryside is spoiled by too many cars.

▲ A result of fewer people using the railways: in 1965 a forlorn tank-engine waited in the yards to be broken up.

◀ The railway station at Dolgellau in Wales stands derelict and deserted, the platform overgrown with grass and the track ripped up. The length of railway line in Britain has been reduced by almost half since the end of World War II.

▶ Holidaymakers climb aboard their charter flight, bound for the sun and the sea. Chartered holidays by 'plane have taken the place of the excursion train in giving people new opportunities for travel.

Railways today

Two contrasting aspects of railways today.

◀ The popular Festiniog 'toy' railway in Wales. In many countries locomotives are preserved in museums, and steam railways have become tourist attractions.

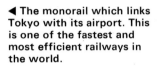

◀ The monorail which links Tokyo with its airport. This is one of the fastest and most efficient railways in the world.

The reign of the steam locomotive lasted over a hundred years. Today it has been overtaken in most countries by electric and diesel engines.

The first railway to run on electricity was opened in 1881 near Berlin, and today railways in many parts of the world are being electrified. The longest electric railway runs from Moscow to Irkutsk, on the Trans-Siberian Railway, a distance of 5,215 kilometres.

The first diesel locomotive was also made in Germany, in 1912, but the diesel revolution really began when the *Electro-Motive No. 103*, a freight diesel, was built in America in 1939. In a year's trials it covered 133,550 kilometres in extreme temperatures and at altitudes of over 3,000 metres. Diesel and electric locomotives need fewer men to work them and are cleaner than steam engines; as it became more difficult to find suitable coal to fuel steam engines, they were gradually taken out of service.

▶ A Canadian diesel engine hauls a freight train over a bridge in Ontario. The train carries 'containers' which are suitable for journeys by road, rail, sea or air. Now that passenger traffic is declining railways rely increasingly on freight, and particularly container traffic, to make money.

Index